I0820053

WHEN WILL THERE FINALLY BE PEACE?

Answers to Questions about War, Violence, Refugees, and Reconciliation

Elisabeth Raffauf

ILLUSTRATED BY
Günther Jakobs

TRANSLATED BY
Patrick Conlin

Paulist Press
New York / Mahwah, NJ

ELISABETH RAFFAUF is a psychologist who works in private practice in Cologne, Germany. She has helped develop an educational series for children's radio and has hosted a children's news program. She has also written parenting guides and educational books.

GÜNTHER JAKOBS is an illustrator for children's and young adults' books. He studied philosophy and graphic design with a focus on illustration. He lives in Münster, Germany.

Cover image by Günther Jakobs
Cover and book design by Lynn Else
Expert advice: Jana Kämmer

Library of Congress Control Number: 2024946095

ISBN 978-0-8091-5729-7 (paperback)
ISBN 978-0-8091-8897-0 (ebook)

Published by Paulist Press
997 Macarthur Boulevard
Mahwah, NJ 07430
www.paulistpress.com

Printed and bound in the
United States of America
by Versa Press, Inc.
Peoria, Illinois
April 2025

Translator's Note

Children are curious by nature. They take in all that is around them. There is a great deal of talk today about the wars in Ukraine, Palestine, Sudan, and elsewhere around the world. Naturally, children have questions about these big issues. Elisabeth Raffauf has provided answers and, more importantly, ways for adults to have conversations with children about these daunting topics.

Within these pages, you will read real questions and responses from real children who have experienced war firsthand. Children from Syria, Ukraine, and Afghanistan share their stories of escape and survival. These stories and comments are opportunities for children in relatively peaceful countries to begin to understand what war is like and thus begin to empathize more deeply with those suffering through war.

Because this book was originally written and released in Germany, some of the stories center on the refugee experience in Europe. Europe is much closer geographically to these current wars than North America is. Therefore, some of the stories may be seen as a window into the experience of those fleeing war and moving to Germany or other European countries. Of course, many refugees also come to North America, and refugees from the Middle East or Ukraine face some similar challenges there (difficult travel, new language, culture, school, friends, and more), but some challenges might be unique to refugees coming to Europe (sailing in an inflatable boat across the Aegean Sea, for example). However, many of those experiences are shared by refugees who eventually end up in North America after flying out of a European nation (rather than settling there as some in this book did). Thus, refugees in North America do share some of the same experiences as you will read here, but their journeys are also different in important ways.

With the focus of this book being on war and peace in countries such as Ukraine, Syria, and Afghanistan, there is little mention of those who flee from other forms of oppression, such as Latin Americans who come to the United States in search of better opportunities, more available food and housing, or to escape corrupt and unjust governments. These people face different challenges in their home countries, in their journeys, and in their lives within their new country. These challenges are outside of the scope of this book, with its focus on the wars that grab headlines.

These tend to be the wars that children hear and wonder about, whether they are from North America or Europe. The stories, comments, and questions in this book are from actual children in elementary and middle school. I hope that by bringing this book to an English-speaking audience, children in North America can develop and expand their empathy and understanding to other people—children and adults—who are facing war and asking, "When will there finally be peace?"

Patrick Conlin

What does peace mean?

Have you ever thought about what peace means? For those of us who may have always lived safely and protected, war seems far away, and peace is taken for granted. It's normal for us to walk freely down the street, play, shop, and more without having to think about whether something might happen. Without having to look around to see if some hostile enemy is following us. Without having to constantly worry about an alarm siren warning us to take shelter quickly.

Peace means a life without fear. In this first meaning of the word, peace means that there is no war, that people can live together without fighting or killing each other.

For many people, peace means more than just the absence of war. It means people are free and not oppressed by the government or by other people.

Hunger and poverty are also not peaceful conditions to live in. These prevent peace because there is a constant struggle for survival. Peace also means that people are treated fairly and that no one has to be afraid of being treated badly because of their skin color, religion, language, or gender.

Peace means equal opportunities for boys and girls too.

Children who constantly experience heated arguments between or with their parents do not live in peace either. Therefore, peace also means having families who love each other.

For me, peace means happiness.
Shahad, 13, fled Syria at the age of 3.
For me, peace means that no one in my family has died.
Leila, 14, fled Syria at the age of 12.
Here was peace. You could go out at night. There were good cars. The roads were good too. Everything was new. I was happy that I could finally go to school in peace and that nothing would happen on the way there.
Mohammad was 11 when he arrived in Germany after fleeing from Afghanistan with his family.

What is war?

War. The word is short and hard. And war itself is hard. Unfortunately, it's not always short. If you are lucky and grew up in a peaceful country, free from serious conflicts, then you might never have heard the word *war* before and cannot imagine what it really means.

War means that disagreements between groups or countries are no longer being settled with words but with violence, especially armed violence. Many things are destroyed in the process. People are killed. Houses, streets, and entire cities are ruined.

There are different types of war, depending on who starts the war, why it is fought, and which groups are at war with each other.

In wars of aggression, the rulers of one country decide to attack another country. They then order their soldiers to invade that country and attack it with bombs and missiles.

Defensive wars are different. In these, a country or group defends itself and fights back against an attack instead of directly surrendering.

There are also civil wars. These are wars when two different enemy groups within a country fight each other. For example, they both might claim a certain area for themselves. Another example is when an armed group might fight against the government and military of its own country, possibly because they want to overthrow the government and take power themselves.

What is a soldier?

People in the military are called soldiers. They are part of an army or another similar group, meaning they are in an armed troop or an official of such troops.

Soldiers wear uniforms.

In their training, they learn how to act in war, how to use their weapons, and how to fight.

War means that people die. People are separated from their families. You're afraid of the people who started the war. You cry a lot in war. The worst thing is that you have to flee your home country and that bombs could fall at any time.

Setayes, 10, was 3 when his family fled from Afghanistan to Germany.

For me, war means that a lot of bad things happen. Dead people, loud noises, screams. I heard so many noises. That's why New Year's Eve is so hard for me. It reminds me.

Fatima, 12, was 5 when she fled to Germany from Afghanistan with her parents and six siblings.

What happens when a war starts?

Usually, a lot of anger and unrest has already occurred between countries or groups before they go to war. There are different opinions that cannot come together. Compromise no longer seems possible. So, one group decides to use violence to force its opinion or claim on the other group. One group attacks the other group with weapons, or one country invades another with force to conquer it. Tanks roll out, bombs drop, rockets fire. Citizens are frightened, terrified, and don't know what to do or how best to protect themselves. Should they flee quickly? Do they want to stay in their homes? Can they even stay? Do they have to fight for themselves? Should they stay and fight?

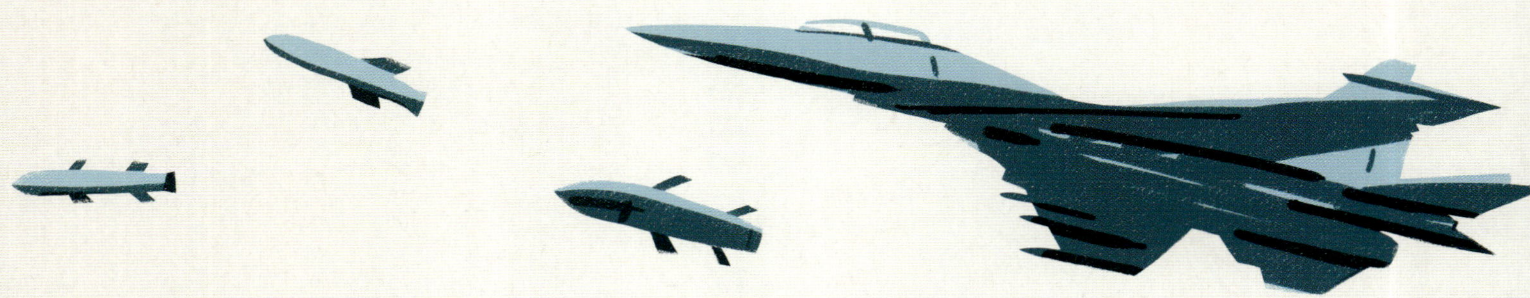

What was it like when war broke out in your area?

I woke up because I heard explosions. At first, I thought it was fireworks. But after the second explosion, I realized it wasn't fireworks. Our family panicked. We started gathering everything and packing. But then we decided to stay.

Nika, 9, lives in Ukraine.

I woke up by myself. Then I asked my parents why they hadn't woken up my little brother and me. The answer was that war had broken out. I was shocked and afraid.

Chloe, 10, fled from Ukraine.

Why is there war?

That is really a difficult question. War sometimes happens when leaders of countries or regions cannot come to an agreement using words. Sometimes they happen when these leaders don't accept that there are people who think differently and want to live differently from themselves. If these people don't act the way the leaders want, the leaders force them to do so with violence.

Sometimes wars happen because the leaders of one country want to expand their rule to become even more powerful than they already are. They try to do this by conquering another country. Of course, no other country wants to give up part of its territory or the people living there. The conquering army therefore uses weapons, and the country that is being conquered fights back. This is war.

How long does a war last?

War always lasts far too long for the people who find themselves caught in the middle of it. That much is clear. People die every day, every hour, every minute in war. Houses and cities are destroyed.

If you take all the wars of the last two hundred years and averaged out how long they lasted, you would get a rough figure of fifteen months per war. That's quite a long time. Short wars are therefore unusual, but still happen. The shortest war was the British-Zanzibar War. It only lasted thirty-eight minutes. The longest was a war between the Netherlands and the Isles of Scilly off the coast of England. They simply forgot to sign a peace treaty though, so the war officially lasted 355 years.

I found out because my mother was so upset. It was at night. We heard lots of noises. My mother said, "Oh God, it's war." Then we fled. The Taliban made loud noises with the bombs.

Fatima, 12, fled Afghanistan when she was 5.

What is a terrorist?

The word *terrorist* comes from the Latin word *terrere*, which means "to frighten or terrify someone." Terrorists are people who spread fear. They frighten others and want to intimidate them. They do this mainly by acting unpredictably. They plan attacks on people, buildings, and other completely random targets. It is impossible to predict when and where they will carry out their next attack.

Terrorists have attacked soccer stadiums, buildings, and Christmas markets around the world. This is very scary for people because these attacks are so disorienting. There is often nothing that could have calculated or predicted such an attack.

This is exactly what terrorists want.

Their goal is for everyone to live the way the terrorists think is the "right way." In order to make this happen, they want to scare people so much that they constantly feel threatened and even mistrust each other. Terrorists want people to think, "Anyone might be my enemy."

Why do people do this?

There are probably several reasons: Terrorists often live through violence, rejection, and oppression as children. They might carry this with them for their entire lives. If you were treated badly as a child, it might be difficult for you to love yourself or others. You might not learn how to empathize with others. Those who have often been put down and humiliated feel small and less than others. To get rid of this feeling, terrorists try to humiliate others, gain power over them, or even kill them. They make themselves feel big by making others feel small. Many terrorists have grown up in poor conditions.

They live in poor parts of cities where there is violence, poverty, and no opportunities for education. They feel left out and ignored by society. This can lead them to hate other people more and more.

Religion is sometimes said to be another reason for terrorism, when terrorist groups say

that they are carrying out such attacks in the name of their god. Radical religious leaders have forcefully convinced them over years that this is what their god wants. Further, many even believe that by fighting against people of different beliefs they will enter a better world after they die. This lets them feel important, a feeling they might not have known in their lives until that time. By believing that they are acting on behalf of their god, they believe they don't have to take responsibility for their actions. Some are even prepared to die for their beliefs.

Another cause for terrorist attacks is when some people have political ideas that are completely different than their society's, so they attack people in that society.

What happens to people in war?

As you can imagine, people don't do well during a war. There is no longer a normal, everyday life because people constantly have to look out for a bomb that might fall on their house or on their friends' houses. Schools and stores close, and most people won't dare to go outside. Sometimes the government even forbids people to go out onto the streets. Depending on how close the war is, people may hear bombs, alarms, and sirens. Then people have to hide out in nearby shelters, such as basements or subways. They often have to spend the night there, sometimes with many other people. Of course, people are afraid. Afraid that their houses might be attacked, that a loved one might be killed, or that something might happen to them.

In the early days of a war, many people are stunned by the fact that there really is a war and unsure of what this means for them. At first, they may not even be able to decide what to do or how to get on with their lives. Many go back and forth between the idea of staying at home and packing their bags and fleeing. Some don't know where to go and can't imagine leaving their homes and everything dear that belongs to them.

What does war mean to you?

War for me is explosions, alarms, helicopters, and not sleeping well.

Nastja, 10, fled from Ukraine.

War is alarms on the news. When we turn the news off, I feel calmer.

Dasha, 10, fled from Ukraine.

War means fighting with weapons. Bombs dropping. A bomb could drop on you at any time. Fear.

Samir, 15, was 8 when his family fled from Afghanistan.

What about the people from the attacking country?

The people from the country that starts a war and attacks another country naturally have various and different opinions about war. To some extent, this depends on what they know about the war and what they believe about why the war is happening.

Some people think just like their leaders. For example, they might think that the other country needs to be liberated from something terrible or that the country shouldn't be independent but really is a part of their own country. They think that it's good that their soldiers take over the foreign country. Some even think that this is only possible with weapons and violence.

On the other hand, many people don't think war is good at all. They know that people are being killed and that their own friends or relatives might be killed by the war or have to fight in it where they may also be killed.

People from the attacking country may take to the streets to protest against the war. For example, mothers might make signs that they don't want their older children to go to war. But in many countries, such protests are stopped, attacked, or silenced by their own soldiers or police at the command of the government.

Why do people shoot other people?

It's probably hard for you to imagine that people would kill each other, taking away their right to live. Even if we cannot fully understand this terrible thought, there are various reasons this happens.

Some soldiers shoot because they have been trained to, because they are told to, and because it is part of their job. They have resolved to fight for their country and defend it if their commander orders them to—even with weapons.

Others do so out of a deeply held belief, for example, about how people should and should not live. They believe that people who don't think like them have no right to live. Some terrorists justify their actions like this.

Often, soldiers are encouraged to fight by their leaders.

But it sometimes happens that people cause chaos. They look for a place where they can just shoot at random. They do so because they are completely unhappy themselves. They want to make a statement and draw attention to themselves through their actions.

Some feel oppressed and want to feel that they have control and power through such acts. They may also feel angry about injustice, despair about their own lives, and hatred toward others that can lead to people killing others.

Some people were trained to fight and use weapons as children. Some were even forced to do so. Humanitarian aid organizations are trying to help these so-called child soldiers to lead a different, peaceful life. Some, for example, enable them to learn a true profession.

What about two classmates from different countries fighting on the playground or somewhere else?

If two children from different, opposing countries are fighting on the school playground, it might seem like a bad idea to get in the middle of it. On one hand, you might want to walk away and have nothing to do with it. On the other hand, it might bother you, and you might feel that it's not fair. You might even be friends with both of them. "What do kids here have to do with the war?" you ask yourself. Other kids might ask themselves the same thing.

Let's imagine that Konstantin is from a country that is being attacked by the country that Katrina is from. They meet each other and begin arguing. In the argument with Katrina, Konstantin painfully remembers what is happening to his country because of Katrina's homeland. He has heard a lot of bad things from his parents about Katrina's native country and the people there. He doesn't know which side she's on. Does she think that what her country's soldiers are doing to his country is good?

Since Katrina has relatives and friends there, Konstantin sees her as representing the country that is inflicting so much pain on his own relatives and friends in his own homeland.

However, you don't know that Katrina really agrees with what those soldiers from her country are doing. Maybe she is just echoing what she hears from her parents or other relatives. They might watch or read news from their own country, and what they hear there might be different than what Konstantin and his family hear from their own country.

It's complicated. You're on the outside, but you don't want to see them fight.

You could ask them whether they themselves really like the violence that soldiers and war are causing. Maybe they would both say that the war is dumb. Then you could talk about it. In any case, you could ask your teacher—maybe even with some of your classmates—if you could talk about the war in class soon.

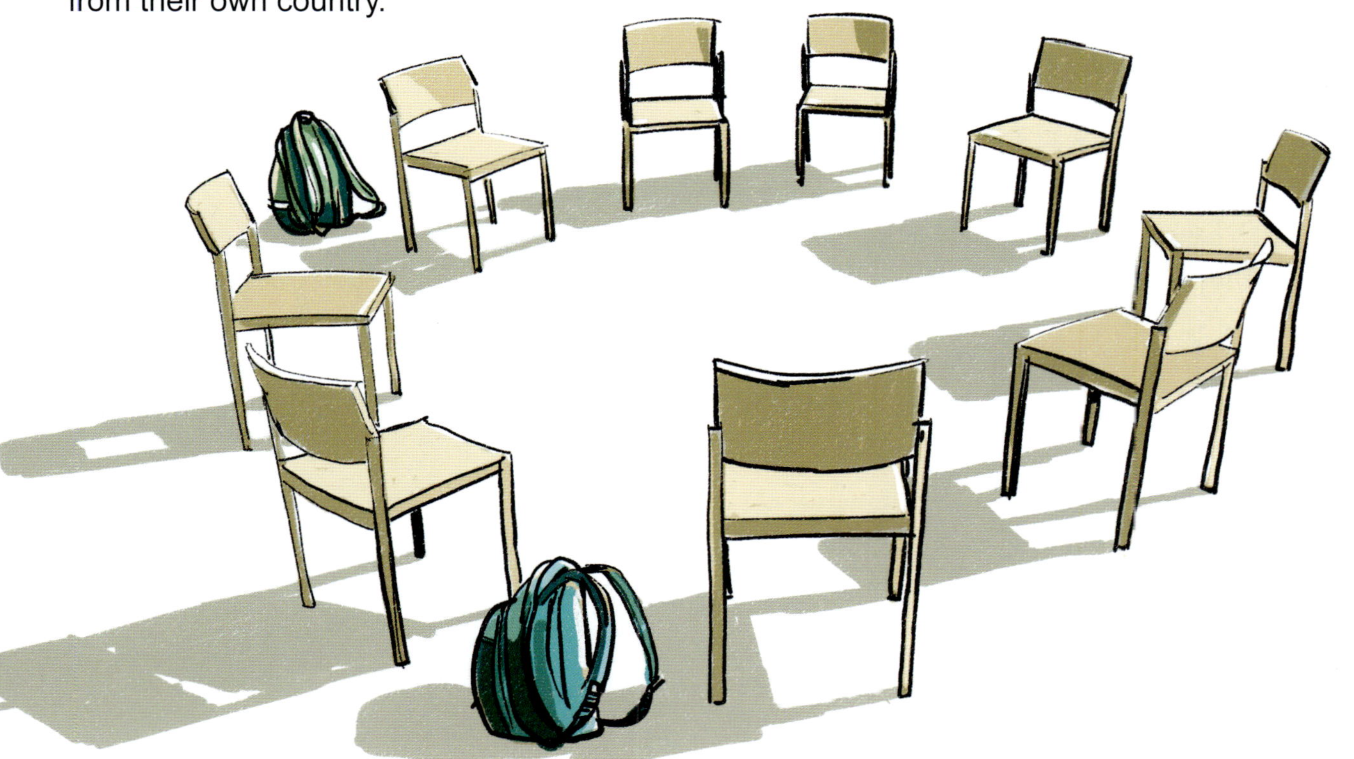

What is allowed in war?

Even in war, there are rules. These are laid down in international law. Next to the law of peace, or international humanitarian law, the law of war is laid out in the Geneva Conventions, one of the most important treaties in international law. It allows a state that is attacked to defend itself. It also explains when another country or alliance may or may not intervene in a war from the outside.

If there is a war, the soldiers of one country may fight the soldiers of another country as well as attack its military buildings. However, it is forbidden to attack or capture civilians. Hospitals, paramedics, and schools are also not to be shot at.

International law also stipulates that prisoners of war, meaning soldiers who are captured by the enemy during the war, must be treated in a humane manner. They must not be tortured; they must have enough to eat and drink; and they must be given the opportunity to contact their families.

Of course, it is never "humane" when people are killed, regardless of whether they are soldiers or civilians. However, these distinctions are made to protect at least some people, specifically those who are not armed.

Unfortunately, not all countries always follow these rules, even if they have signed international treaties to do so.

INTERNATIONAL LAW

International law is an agreement that all countries in the world must follow. This law was created by the United Nations, a group of representatives from each nation. Nearly every country in the world, 193 countries, have signed this agreement.

International law defines how countries should treat each other by defining what rights and obligations nations have toward each other. It is about protecting each country and respecting the borders of others.

Here are two examples:

"Each country may determine for itself how the people there live. No other country may interfere in the internal issues of another country."

"Violence between countries is prohibited. This means no country may attack another country."

CIVILIAN

The word *civilian* refers to every person who isn't a soldier. This includes bakers, teachers, doctors, and many others. Obviously, all children are civilians. In a war, civilians must not be deliberately attacked. They are under special protection.

What is the United Nations?

The United Nations, or UN, is an important international organization. Most countries in the world are members of the UN. It was founded after World War II to ensure peace in the world. As an independent organization, its goal is to act as a mediator between countries when there are conflicts.

The UN is committed to ensuring that its members live together in friendship and that human rights are respected.

The most important group within the UN is the UN Security Council. There are five countries that are permanent members: The United States, Russia, China, the United Kingdom, and France. The other countries alternate in holding the other seats. They are only temporary members. The five permanent members are very powerful, as they have the right to veto decisions. This means that each of these five countries can oppose a joint decision of the council. The decision would then be blocked and not go forward, even if the majority of the other countries were in favor of it.

What happens if a country or group doesn't follow the rules?

If everyone always followed international law, there would be no wars at all. After all, if you're not attacked, you don't have to defend yourself, so there wouldn't even be defensive wars, which—unlike wars of aggression—are permitted under international law.

If a country doesn't abide by the agreements of international law, several organizations seek to ensure justice is done. One such organization is the International Criminal Court in The Hague, a city in the Netherlands. Among other things, people who have committed war crimes can be tried and punished there. Such criminals may be imprisoned for many years. This applies to individual soldiers as well as commanders of troops and leaders of nations. For example, a leader might give the order to attack another country or to kill, injure, or torture civilians, or to bomb hospitals, schools, and homes.

In such a case, the International Court of Justice sends its own staff to the war zone. The staff members look for evidence as to whether the leaders of the attacking country knew about the war crimes, or perhaps even ordered them. If enough evidence is found, the International Court of Justice can put them on trial. If they are found guilty, this court can punish them too. However, for this to happen, the country in which the person is located must first hand them over to the International Court of Justice.

Why not just kill, or at least arrest, the leader of a country that starts a war?

Many people think this when they realize that a head of state is responsible for so many people dying and so many cities being destroyed.

But it is forbidden to kill someone, no matter how much you hate them. Everyone has the right to a fair trial. The United Nations has laid this out in international laws regarding human rights. And, of course, some people fiercely support these leaders within their own countries, so they guard and protect the leaders. The leaders themselves know that some people may want to attack and kill them.

Another problem is that there are no "world police" who can turn on their sirens, ring the doorbell, and just arrest the rulers or their followers. Invading the country with tanks and soldiers to confront the person is not an option either. International law forbids this, because then you would be doing exactly what the other leader is doing—attacking another country.

But it may be possible to prosecute the person later, if it can be proven that the head of the country is guilty of war crimes or crimes against humanity. The police in their own country could then arrest them. If the person flees to another country, that country could extradite them—send them off under arrest—to the International Court of Justice.

Is war coming to us too?

When there is a terrorist attack or a war, reporters from all over the world cover the news online, on TV, on the radio, or in print. The stories shock and terrify people. Many wonder whether there could be a war or terrorist attack in their own country. No one can know the future with certainty.

Some people worry that there won't be enough food if a war starts, so they start buying supplies. Others ask themselves where they could go and what they would do if a war came to their country.

Experts who study and analyze wars all agree: the probability of war coming to North America or the European Union is low. One of the main reasons for this is that the United States, Canada, and most European countries are part of an important military alliance called NATO. This is an alliance between thirty-two European and North American countries in which they have all agreed that they would help each other militarily if another member nation is attacked. Any country that would attack Germany, for example, would have to also deal with the United States, the United Kingdom, and twenty-nine other countries. It's all for one and one for all. Rulers of hostile countries, therefore, must think very carefully about this.

WHAT IS NATO?

NATO stands for the North Atlantic Treaty Organization. This is a political and military alliance that has thirty-two democratically governed countries as members. *Democratic* means that decisions in the country are made by elections in which the people cast their vote.

The goals of NATO are peace and freedom. The NATO countries have pledged to support one another militarily if one of them is attacked.

The member nations discuss among themselves how they want to behave in the event of conflicts or attacks.

Following the outbreak of war in Ukraine, Finland and Sweden, who were not part of this alliance before, became members.

Terrorist attacks are also rare in the United States and Canada. We tend to remember the big ones that have occurred in the past, such as the terrorist attacks on September 11, 2001. However, scientists say that a person is more likely to be struck by lightning or be killed by a poisonous mushroom than to experience such an attack themselves.

What if I'm afraid?

When you hear about a war or a terrorist attack and see pictures and videos of ruined houses and desperate people, you might feel scared. If so, that's definitely understandable. You aren't alone either. Such images are frightening, and fear is an appropriate feeling in response. Some people might say, "You don't have to be afraid." They might mean well, but such sayings don't always make us feel less anxious. Sometimes it's more helpful to take a closer look at our feelings than just dismissing them immediately.

Fear is like our emotional alarm system, deeply rooted in us as humans. It's triggered when a danger threatens us. Fear is like a warning signal that we need to protect ourselves. If a car is coming toward you, your instincts kick in without thinking, and you jump out of the way immediately. If you see horrific pictures of disasters on TV or the internet, you might feel threatened yourself. Your alarm system is triggered even though there is no immediate danger to you personally.

A war and pictures or stories of an attack can cause fear. That's when it's most important to share and talk about your feelings with people you trust rather than just bottling them up. This can help since others can share your burden.

What helps when I'm afraid?

If you talked about your feelings of fear with other people whom you trust, you'd see that your feelings are perfectly understandable. War and terrorism are scary. Many other people feel afraid too.

Talking about your feelings has another advantage. You won't feel alone with your fear; you can share it with others.

Drawing a picture of your feelings or writing them down in a journal can also help you. Do they feel like a dark cloud? Or like a big menacing giant? You could even draw what you imagine the world would be like without such darkness, when the sun can finally shine over peace. This can provide a new perspective on your fear.

Words, pictures, or even music are ways of symbolizing a feeling that might help us understand our feelings better and process them.

Many times, it's hard to define exactly what we're feeling or what we're afraid of. That is why it is helpful to try to understand our feelings and what triggers them.

For example, learning that your country is part of the NATO alliance with many other countries or that a terrorist attack is less likely than a lightning strike might reduce your fear. Or you might be reassured by finding out more about how politicians in your country are helping to preserve peace both here and around the world. On one hand, it can be a good idea to recognize your fear, to find out what helps you talk about it, and to find out more information about a war. On the other hand, you are also allowed to distract yourself with something fun or something that makes you laugh.

Are soldiers afraid too?

People who fight in a war naturally feel fear too. Fear that they or their comrades will die, fear that they will not be able to defend themselves well, fear that their country will lose and they will be captured, fear that they will not see their families again. Some are afraid that they will have to harm or even kill other people, which they don't really want to do. Some soldiers are even afraid of admitting that they are afraid. They have many fears.

At the same time, however, some are proud that they are fighting for their country and defending it. Before soldiers are sent into a war zone, they are prepared by psychologists for what they should expect in war. There are other people who provide help to soldiers, even accompanying troops in their deployment. Chaplains are religious clergy whom soldiers can turn to for support. It's important and helpful for soldiers to be able to share their fears too.

What does it mean to be a refugee?

Being a refugee means fleeing from your country and having to leave your home. This isn't like going on a vacation, because you are forced to leave. As you can imagine, no one would want to just leave behind their home, maybe forever, and go on a dangerous journey to a foreign country. For them, this is a life-or-death decision, a question of survival and a safe future.

Some people leave their country because of great poverty that leads to hungry families. People can't find jobs, and they don't know how they will be able feed themselves or their families. Other people are persecuted by the government or police because they have different opinions on politics or society. Others face discrimination in their homeland because of their religion or their sexual or gender orientation. Many people leave their country because of war there. They fear for their lives and their families.

The journey itself can take a very long time. Sometimes people have to spend the night outside in the cold or go without enough to eat or drink. Many people cannot simply get on a train or a plane and travel to another country, either because they don't have enough money or because there might be no trains or planes out of their country. This might happen because the government forbids it, sometimes even shutting down roads and bridges.

It might also be difficult to escape because some countries limit or even forbid refugees from entering. They might send refugees back to their original country immediately. Sometimes refugees might have to pass through countries that are at war in order to finally reach safety.

Many people fleeing war, especially from Africa or Syria, sail across the Mediterranean Sea in small inflatable rafts that aren't meant to cross such waters. They pay a lot of money to the owners of the boats, but there is no guarantee that they will make it across the Mediterranean alive. Many people die along the way.

Others, especially from Latin America, cover thousands of miles on foot, passing through unsafe and dangerous areas along the way. Some are robbed or even attacked. For many refugees, escape means uncertainty and danger.

Where are refugees fleeing to?

Most refugees are going to areas within their own country unaffected by the war. These people are called internal refugees. Others flee to nearby countries and still others to countries that are far away from their homeland.

Depending on where they arrive, refugees might be treated very differently. They might have different rights than natural citizens in some countries, or they might face discrimination within a community. Sometimes countries have different laws for the protection of refugees. Many refugees from the Middle East or Africa want to flee to North America or to a European country. They hope to find work and a secure future there. Many refugees from Syria, Afghanistan, or Sudan come across the Mediterranean Sea into Greece in those dangerous rubber rafts. They often end up in a refugee camp, cut off from the rest of the life of the country. Refugees are forced to stay in camps until the reasons why they left their country are recognized as legitimate by the country they are going into.

For some refugees, this process takes years. In Europe, many refugees arrive in the same few cities. The countries of the European Union (EU) would have enough room for all of their incoming refugees if they were evenly spread out across the countries, but the countries can't agree on how to share this responsibility. Some countries don't want to accept any refugees, or only a few, so many people have to wait in refugee camps. Many refugees are children, some who might be alone without their families. They face many challenges when they're stuck like this. Even if local schools accept them, they might not speak the language. Other places might not have enough room for them. They don't feel welcome, and they don't know where to go.

Samir's story

I remember a stranger touching my hand on the boat. I screamed so loudly! Then the man suggested I put my hand in the water to calm down. Then a fish swam past my hand. It was only a small one, but I thought it was a shark! So, I screamed even louder.

Setayesh, 10, Samir's sister who was 3 at the time.

Samir was eight years old when he fled to Germany from Afghanistan with his parents and six siblings. One morning, his parents told him that a terrorist group called the Taliban had attacked the city and placed landmines nearby. Samir had always been afraid of the Taliban and the possibility of war. Now that the Taliban was directly threatening their family, his parents decided to flee. Samir and his siblings were very sad about leaving their home. They even had to say goodbye to their grandpa who couldn't flee with them.

They were afraid of moving to Germany. They imagined big, fast-paced cities with skyscrapers and people speaking a language they couldn't understand. The escape itself took several months. First, they took a bus to Iran where they stayed in a home for refugees. They had to share a room with others who were escaping Afghanistan. A month later, they started for Turkey. That wasn't easy. The Iranian soldiers wanted to send him and his family back to Afghanistan. It worked out though, but they had to cross the mountains of northern Iran in the snow. Samir sat on a horse with his mother and sister. His older brothers and father had to trudge through the snow across the mountains.

Finally, they made it to Istanbul in Turkey where they stayed at another refugee center for another month. Then they continued their journey across the sea to Greece in an inflatable boat. The boat was very small, and sixty people were in it. Everyone was crowded together. The boat started to break down while they were onboard. Water came in. They had to scoop out the water with a bucket and throw their bags overboard. Samir later learned that many other refugees in similar boats died along their journey.

In Greece, the refugees were met by police officers who gave them blankets and took them to a camp where they were able to eat. The police told them to stay there, but they wanted to continue to Germany. A few days later, they took a train from Greece to Germany, passing through several countries along the way. In Germany, they were sent from one city to another. For eleven months they lived in a sports arena with many other people, where no one had their own room. Samir's mother cooked outside the arena. Eventually, they met a German couple named Jörg and Alexe. They invited the whole family to their home, and they gave them all gifts since it was Christmas. Jörg and Alexe later helped them find a nice apartment with enough room for them all. They've lived there ever since.

What questions do refugee children ask?

What is it like to be a kid in a foreign country?

When refugee children arrive in a foreign country, they often feel insecure. They don't know anyone, they don't have any friends there, and they don't speak the language. Everything is strange and unknown. Every street, every building, every apartment, the people, the smells, the food, the culture is new. At first, some families live in buildings specifically for refugees with many other families. They are often cramped together, forced to share small spaces with strangers. Others might live in a former hotel that has been turned into refugee housing, or still others live with a host family.

Some children can go to school online and continue learning from their own teachers in their home countries even after fleeing. This is a great support for those students, as it lets them stay in contact with their home country and their friends.

Learning a new language in a new country is a big challenge for anyone. If you don't understand anything and can't communicate with others, you feel like a stranger to everyone. Learning a new language takes time. Before they master the new language, some children have to go to school, and they have to communicate with their new classmates by pointing at things and using gestures. Thankfully, they can at least play together without needing to speak the same language.

Refugee children think about their homes and their friends there a lot. The vast majority wish that they could go back to their own homes.

What happens to kids' toys when they flee their country?

Most children can only take a few personal items with them when they flee. They can't carry a lot, especially if they must go a long way or travel by foot at times. Often, they leave home without a lot of warning and can only pack a small backpack with just what they need. They have to leave most of their toys at home. Some children might take a doll or electronic toy or device with them. Others don't bring any toys with them at all.

What do refugee children wish for?

I wish I could go home and see my friends again.

Chloe, 10, fled from Ukraine.

My dream is to be able to forget the war.

Nastja, 10, fled from Ukraine.

I wish that my country would be safe. That the Taliban would leave. When I'm older and a math professor, I'll go back to Afghanistan and teach college there.

Saifudin, 20, was 13 when he fled Afghanistan with his family.

I wish there had never been a war, so I wouldn't have had to flee. I wish that the Taliban would leave Afghanistan alone so that we could live in peace. The Taliban are the people who started the war. They were jealous of the people. That's why they started the war.

Setayesh, 10, fled Afghanistan when she was 3.

Enough is enough. We just want to live in peace.

Mohammad, 18, was 11 when he fled from Afghanistan.

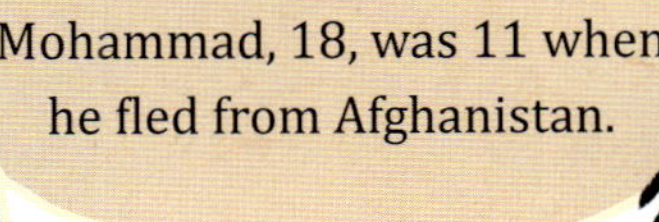

I wish the war would end. I would like to see my family who stayed behind—my aunt, my uncle, and my grandpa.

Raghda, 16, was 6 when she fled from Syria.

How can we help?

Images of terrible events like war or people fleeing their countries can be very upsetting. Many people feel afraid and powerless. The feeling of not being able to do anything can be almost paralyzing. Of course, we can't end a war by ourselves. Government leaders must end it. But that doesn't mean there's nothing we can do to help people. When we help others, we actually help ourselves too. If you help, even in small ways, you realize you don't need to feel so powerless and helpless. We can set an example for others.

During a crisis or a war, you might see signs on people's houses or businesses or even held up by marchers in the street saying things like "Refugees Welcome!" When the war broke out in Ukraine, many schools even had students paint Ukrainian flags or doves symbolizing peace. Many people had signs or wrote messages such as "Stop the war!" or "Stop Putin!" Some classrooms or houses had signs like this on the doors or walls or flew Ukrainian flags. They gave the same message to everyone who walked past, including refugees: "We want peace." Refugees learned that they had allies and that their classmates at school were on their side.

People also show solidarity with refugees on social media. They post messages or share stories to bring awareness to the situation. They call on politicians in their own country to take action.

When I went to school for the first time, I was paired up with another student. She looked out for me and helped me speak the language. I was teased a lot because I didn't speak like other kids. I even had to repeat first grade. Things got better, but I was still teased for being too childish and believing in fairy tales.

Setayesh, 10 years old.

You might even have a classmate who is a refugee, or you might sometime in the future. Even if they don't speak the same language at first, there are a lot of ways you can make them feel welcome. You can smile at them and invite them to play at recess. Maybe you and your friends could come up with a sort of "sign language" to communicate with such classmates. For example, you might pretend to dribble a ball to say, "Let's play basketball." You could also teach each other new words. Ask them how to say "hello," "thank you," or "let's play!" in their language and teach them how to say it in English. They might sound funny at first, but remember, you might sound funny to them too!

You could also help by donating clothes or toys to organizations that give them to refugees. Certain organizations might have collection centers nearby that help refugees in your country or that send donations to other places around the world. You might even be able to organize a local fundraiser, like a bake sale or car wash, and donate the proceeds to a charity that helps refugees.

There might be protests and demonstrations that you can participate in. Make sure you ask your parents about this first. They might even know where such events are taking place and would know which ones you could go to as a family. Your friends and other family members might want to come with you too. You might make signs with antiwar slogans or other positive sayings. It's more fun and effective to do so together. Your friends and family might have other ideas about how you could help.

I'm lonely.
Shahad, 13, fled Syria at 3.

People sound funny in a foreign country. There are so many languages and accents.
Raghda, 16, fled Syria at 6.

What can other countries do against war?

When there is a war somewhere in the world, other countries are called upon to react to this situation. They might say, "It's none of our business; it's their war; we won't get involved." But they might also consider how they can take a stand and support the country they think is right. If and how a country responds depends on many factors. These include how close the countries are to one another, how economically connected they are, whether refugees are coming into their own country, or how threatened they feel by the war themselves.

A country might impose sanctions against the government or the leaders of the country responsible for the war. Sanctions are like punishments. For example, your country might freeze any bank accounts there that belong to the leaders, preventing them from accessing that money. A country might block travel to and from the attacking country or stop selling goods to that country. These measures are meant to weaken that country's economy.

On the other hand, your country might send humanitarian aid. This means helping to rebuild schools and hospitals and sending money, medicine, food, clothing, and hygiene items to the war-torn country. We can all welcome and accept refugees. In addition, your country could send weapons to the country it wants to support. This all has to be done according to international treaties and in cooperation with NATO and other countries.

What do international aid organizations do?

There are many large organizations that provide international aid, including UNICEF—the United Nations Children's Fund—and the Red Cross. There are other smaller organizations as well.

The first thing that such organizations do is collect donations. These might be money or other practical items like water, food, or clothes, depending on what is needed. They might collect things like medicine, blankets, bottled water, or hygiene items like soap, toothpaste, diapers, or tampons. Some organizations, like Doctors Without Borders, send doctors and nurses to crisis areas to provide medical care.

These organizations rely on volunteers, people who work for these organizations without being paid for it. They might collect money or donations in their free time and then, once they have enough, give it to paid employees who can take it overseas. This makes sure that these donations get to where they need to go. In a war, the drivers delivering these supplies face dangerous conditions just to bring help to others.

Not just countries facing war need help; countries affected by natural disasters such as droughts or floods also need humanitarian aid. There are children's organizations that focus on ensuring that children all over the world are safe from violence and exploitation, that they can live healthy lives, that they can go to school, and that they don't need to have a job like adults would.

Aid organizations help a lot, even if there is no war or disaster. They often provide support to poorer countries in Asia, Africa, and Latin America.

How can a war end and peace begin again?

Wars are always unbearable for the people involved. They can no longer live carefree. You can't get used to war. Therefore, the most important questions are: What needs to happen for peace to return? Who can mediate? Does someone have to "win" first? What happens afterward?

Some wars end only when one side has won. In others, the UN or other mediating countries can convince or pressure the warring parties to reach a ceasefire, meaning a stop to the fighting, at least for a time.

The two parties may also realize that they are roughly equal in strength and that neither can really win, so they come to a peace agreement. However a war ends, a solution to the conflict must be negotiated afterward so that people can once again live together in peace, without fear of violence.

Wars usually end when some or all of the warring countries are no longer able to fight. For example, one side might realize that they have little or no chance of maintaining their resistance and continuing to defend themselves. That country might not have enough money or enough soldiers and weapons or the strength or the hope to win.

Of course, it's best when countries can sit down at a table and negotiate peace. Navid Kermani is an author and the winner of the 2015 Peace Prize from the German Publisher's Association. He has written many books on the topics of war and peace. As he put it, "Wars are made by people and can only be ended by people."

What happens to a country after a war?

It's very difficult to predict what will happen in a country after a war. It depends on many factors. One thing is clear: regardless of how it ends or whether there is a "winner" or a "loser," people in both countries have lost a lot. There are destroyed buildings, injured people, and death on both sides.

If the country that was attacked wins, their leaders can now determine how their own people will live. If the attacking country wins, it will be able to dictate the laws and ways of life of the people there. If this happens, the winning country will continue to oppress people, and some people will have to flee. Some refugees might never return to their homes.

Many things need to be rebuilt before life can go back to normal. Water, electricity, internet, and cell phone service need to be restored. Food supplies and stores need to be refilled. Hospitals, schools, bridges, and roads need to be rebuilt. Often the country needs to rely on other countries for this support. When a war ends, working toward peace begins.

People need to look at how they can live together in peace again, how they reconcile with others. Justice must occur so that people can come to terms with what has happened. War crimes need to be reported and investigated.

People will mourn for a long time. They have lost many friends and loved ones; they have seen and experienced terrible things. So many things have been destroyed.

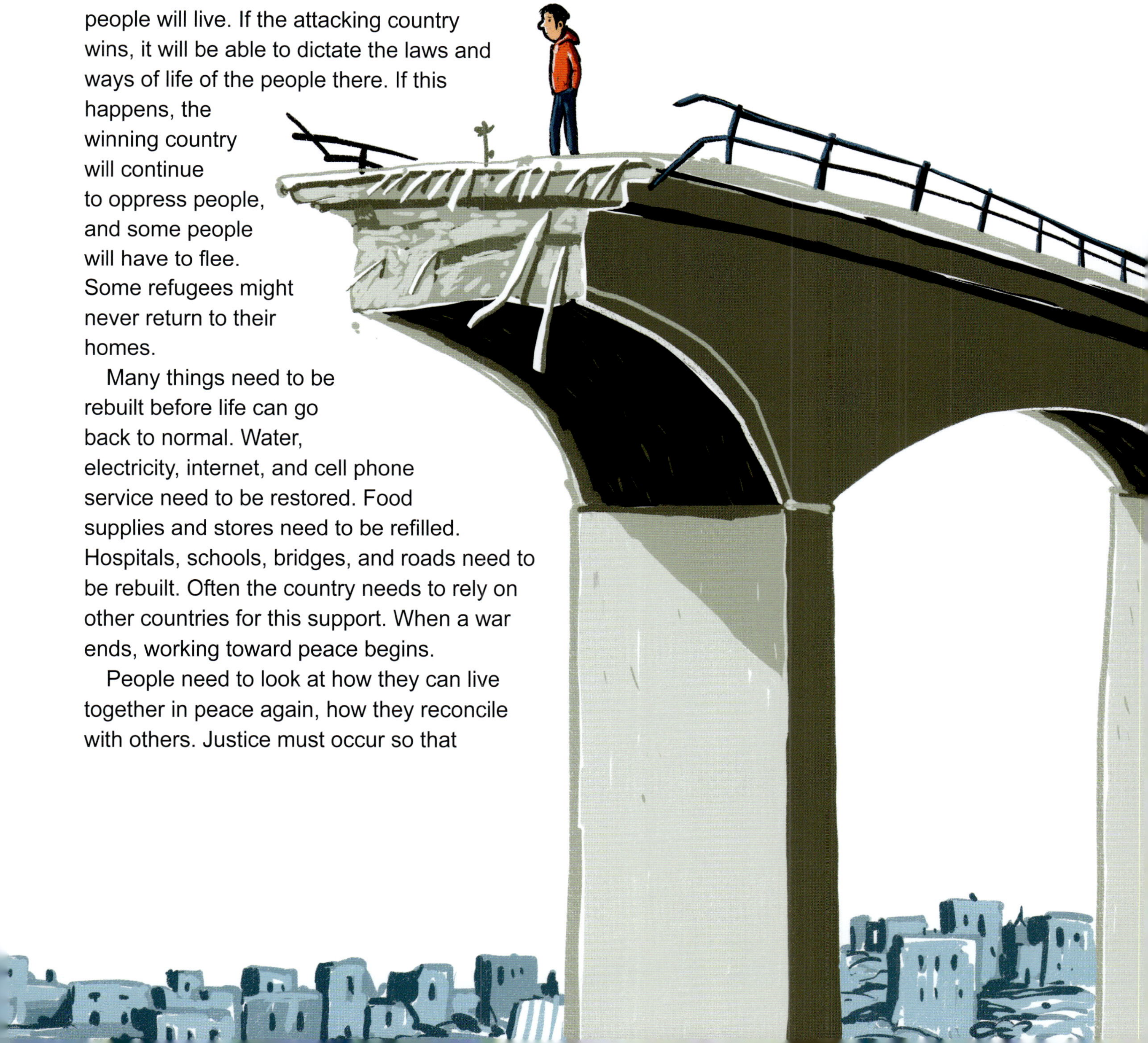

Can we prevent war before it happens?

It would be best if wars didn't happen at all. Some people try to prevent wars. "Peace studies" is a field of research that looks at what is happening politically and socially around the world to understand the conflicts and crises that exist. They see which difficult situations are escalating, how powerful individual governments are, which countries are suffering, which groups are promoting violence, and where differences of opinion are intensifying. They ask which conflicts may be coming next based on injustices, hunger, or powerful groups oppressing weaker groups. These researchers look at all sides to understand how people are feeling, especially when they might feel backed into a corner.

Peace researchers try to find out how countries or groups have dealt with problems in the past. This helps them see what the possibilities for peace are and how they can sit down to negotiate a resolution. From all this information, they can make an educated prediction of whether and where an armed conflict might occur.

These researchers then create reports on these issues, which they pass on to politicians and leaders in their countries. Based on these reports, the governments of the countries can decide whether they should try to mediate a peace treaty, provide other help, or even deploy soldiers to the other country before a war breaks out.

What can we do for peace in our own neighborhoods?

We can promote peace in our own environments by trying to understand each other. We can empathize better with people, even people we don't like, if we learn about their history and the reasons why they act the way they do.

If you are in an argument with someone, approach the other person peacefully and see if you can reach a compromise with them.

Talk about your ideas about peace with others and listen to their ideas. This helps us become more aware of what peace really means and why it's important. If we keep talking with each other about peace, there is less chance of conflict breaking out.

If you see injustice, protest against it, maybe with others from your school, family, or neighborhood. You can talk about peace in school, or your class could write "Peace Letters" to each other with messages of encouragement and hope. For example, you might start a Peace Letter with "I like the way that you...," or "I think you're very good at...," and fill in the rest with something nice about your classmate. Maybe you could even ask your teacher to have a box for these in your classroom.

Peace does not come and stay automatically. We have to do something for peace every day. By talking to each other, resolving arguments, seeking compromises, and reconciling with others, we can all promote peace.

Epilogue

Dear readers,

Children sense everything that is happening around them. It's like they have antennae that pick up vibrations from their families, friends, and the world around them.

When some terrible or tragic event occurs, they might feel like their whole world is falling apart. Some children may express this more easily than others. Words help children make sense of the world. Words are one way to symbolize their feelings. They can think about them, process them, and learn to manage and express them. If children do not have the words to express themselves, they may be able to use their imaginations and storytelling abilities. When children can put something into words, they feel stronger and more secure emotionally. This applies to children's feelings in general, but also to their feelings about difficult, frightening events such as war, violence, and terrorism.

Parents sometimes have the well-intentioned impulse to shield their children from bad news. It's not easy to answer their questions honestly while not scaring them. On the other hand, children have questions, and they deserve answers. If we deflect the question or tell them "Everything is fine" when they sense this isn't true, they are confused. They can perceive that something more is happening than what we are telling them.

This book encourages you to accompany children in their big questions about the state of the world with concrete suggestions on how to approach such topics in an age-appropriate way. You can read individual questions together or let your child read them on their own. You don't need to read the book in order to have these conversations.

The questions in this book all come from real children. The answers are intended to be concrete, kid-friendly ways to gently introduce difficult topics. I wish stimulating and helpful discussions to you and the children around you!

Thank you very much,

- Dasha, Nika, Chloe, Mia, and Nastja for sharing your experiences of the beginning of the war in Ukraine.
- Fatima, Setayesh, Mohammad, Samir, and Saifudin for sharing your painful memories of fleeing from war, and for sharing your hope.
- Raghda, Leila, Shahad, and Ghaib for telling me about your experiences in the war and escape from it, your arrival in Germany, and your ideas on what helps you when you are afraid. When asked what it was like to have our conversation, Shahad replied, "Relieving."
- Nadja Nesterenko for the opportunity to interview your Ukrainian students and for your help translating our conversations.
- Alexe and Jörg for the connection to the Mohammadi family, and for welcoming us into your garden (with waffles!) for the interview.
- Lina Orrego, who put me in touch with Svenja Burger and a Syrian family.
- Svenja Burger, who put me in touch with the Alhassan family and kindly accompanied me to meet with them.
- Martina Klinke, for helping me contact a Syrian family whom you help.
- The entire team at Fischer Publishers.
- Christel Bossbach for the many suggestions in the form of newspaper articles.
- Jana Kämmer for critically, professionally, and sensitively reviewing the text.
- Günter Jakobs for such striking and touching illustrations.
- Julia Scheit from Fischer Children's Publishing for your idea for the book, your confidence in the project, and your many helpful suggestions and comments.
- The people at Paulist Press for their commitment to publishing this book in the United States.
- Patrick Conlin for the wonderful Translator's Note and the sensitive translation.

Thank you all!
Elisabeth Raffauf

Glossary

Here are some explanations for words from the text and for terms you might hear elsewhere.

ALLIANCE
An association of several groups. For example, different countries may have a treaty to support each other in the event of a war.

ANTIAIRCRAFT WEAPONS
Defensive missiles used to protect a country from enemy helicopters, airplanes, or missiles.

ARTILLERY
A long-range weapon that can fire missiles at targets over great distances, such as land-to-air missiles.

ASSASSINATION
An attempt to kill a specific person. This might be a famous person or a political or social leader with whom the attackers disagree.

ATTACK
A violent assault on people or buildings with the aim of destroying them.

CEASEFIRE
An agreement for weapons to stop shooting. This might be done while leaders negotiate peace terms to bring an end to a war, or for a limited time, for example, to provide humanitarian aid or during an important holiday.

CIVILIAN
A person who is not a soldier.

CLUSTER BOMBS
Large bombs that contain many smaller bombs, about the size of a soda can. They are dropped over a large area, and the small bombs hit many targets without aim. The United Nations has called for an end to their use, but the United States has not signed that treaty.

CONSTITUTION
A constitution contains the rules for the government. Many constitutions recognize the rights of all people to be treated equally and not discriminated against.

DEMOCRACY
Literally, this means “rule of the people.” This is a system of government in which the people choose their leaders, are free to express their opinions, and are allowed to assemble.

DEMONSTRATION
A gathering of several people who want to publicly show their opinion on an issue. Usually, people will give speeches and hold signs stating what they want to see happen. For example, there are demonstrations against war.

DRONE
A flying machine with no people on board controlled remotely by a person or computer on the ground. There are drones that take photos or videos from the air, but also large drones that attack people or buildings.

ECONOMY
Everything relating to money within a country. It refers to the production, sale, distribution, and consumption of goods and services.

HUMANITARIAN AID
Humanitarian refers to human beings. This is help given to people in an emergency, like a war or natural disaster.

HUMAN RIGHTS
The rights of all human beings to live, speak, and assemble freely. These are protected by international law. Other international laws deal with the duties and rights of countries during times of peace and war.

INSURRECTION
A group of people who do not agree with the government and try to take power by force, often by a surprise attack. They might use weapons or violence to gain access to political institutions and drive out those in power.

INTERNATIONAL COURT OF JUSTICE
The court that hears disputes between countries. They investigate war crimes and put war criminals on trial.

LAW OF WAR
The part of international law that lays out the rules that all countries and groups should follow during war.

NATO
The North American Treaty Organization. A political-military alliance of thirty-two democratically governed countries who have pledged to support each other if one is attacked. The United States is a member.

NUCLEAR BOMB
Nuclear bombs are among the most dangerous weapons in the world. They kill large numbers of people and contaminate huge areas with radioactive material for years. They destroy all life in the area.

PROTEST
Another word for "opposition." In a democracy, you can protest decisions and issues peacefully by participating in a demonstration or other means.

SALUTE
A show of respect, usually in greeting or farewell. This includes the gesture of raising your hand to your forehead or when soldiers fire their guns in unison to honor a fallen comrade.

SANCTIONS
Measures that are used to punish or enforce certain behavior. Countries usually impose them on other countries. This might make it harder for the other country to sell or buy international goods, thus draining their supplies.

SEXUAL ORIENTATION
This refers to which sex a person feels emotionally and physically attracted to. In some countries, people with certain sexual orientations may face discrimination.

SOCIAL MEDIA
Online services that can be used to exchange information, write messages, or share pictures and videos with the public or specific people. For example, Snapchat, Instagram, TikTok, YouTube, and others.

SOLIDARITY
This refers to the idea of being "together" with others. Individually, it might mean standing up for a friend. On a larger scale, it might mean standing up for an oppressed group.

TAKE A STAND
To take a side on an issue and express your opinion. Standing your ground on an issue means not backing down under pressure to change your view.

TANK
A large, armored vehicle able to move quickly over difficult ground. Some can shoot at targets over two miles away.

TERRORIST
People who carry out attacks on other people in order to make the others afraid. Often, they kill people and themselves in order to impose their political or religious views on others.

VETO RIGHT
The right of certain countries or people to cancel out a winning, majority vote. The president of the United States can veto laws passed by a majority of Congress, for example.

VOLUNTEER
Someone who willingly works without being paid because of a belief in a cause. Examples are volunteer firefighters, those who help elderly people get food and groceries, those who work in an animal shelter, or those who clean up trash.